EASYART

**Kay Barnham, Fiona Mitchell,
Helen Burnford, Philippa Moyle**

SMITHMARK

CONTENTS

EASYART
Paper

CONTENTS

Hints and Tips

You will need different types of paper to make the things in this book — colored paper, wrapping paper, tissue paper, crêpe paper, brown paper, lining paper, paper plates, paper bags, and magazines. It is a good idea to collect them together and keep them in a cardboard box for when you need them.

Before you start working, put on old clothes or an apron to protect your good clothes from splashes of glue or paint. Also, cover your work area with newspaper.

You can use many types of glue for sticking things together but craft glue works best.

Instead of buying thin card you could use the cardboard from an empty box.

Always ask an adult for help when you need to use a craft knife. You can buy round-ended safety scissors from most craft stores.

Collect useful bits and pieces such as string, paper clips, thumbtacks, poster putty, buttons, and sequins.

Snappy Creatures

You need

Scissors

Colored paper

Felt-tip pen   Glue

1 Cut a piece of paper to make it square. Fold the square in half. Then fold each half back on itself to make a fan shape.

The long side will form the creature's mouth.

2 Open out the middle fold and lay it down with the folded sides tucked under. Fold all the corners in toward the middle fold.

3 Close the middle fold with the folded corners inside. Fold the paper in half with the pointed tips together, and make a crease, then unfold it again. Slip your fingers inside the long side.

Short side

Long side

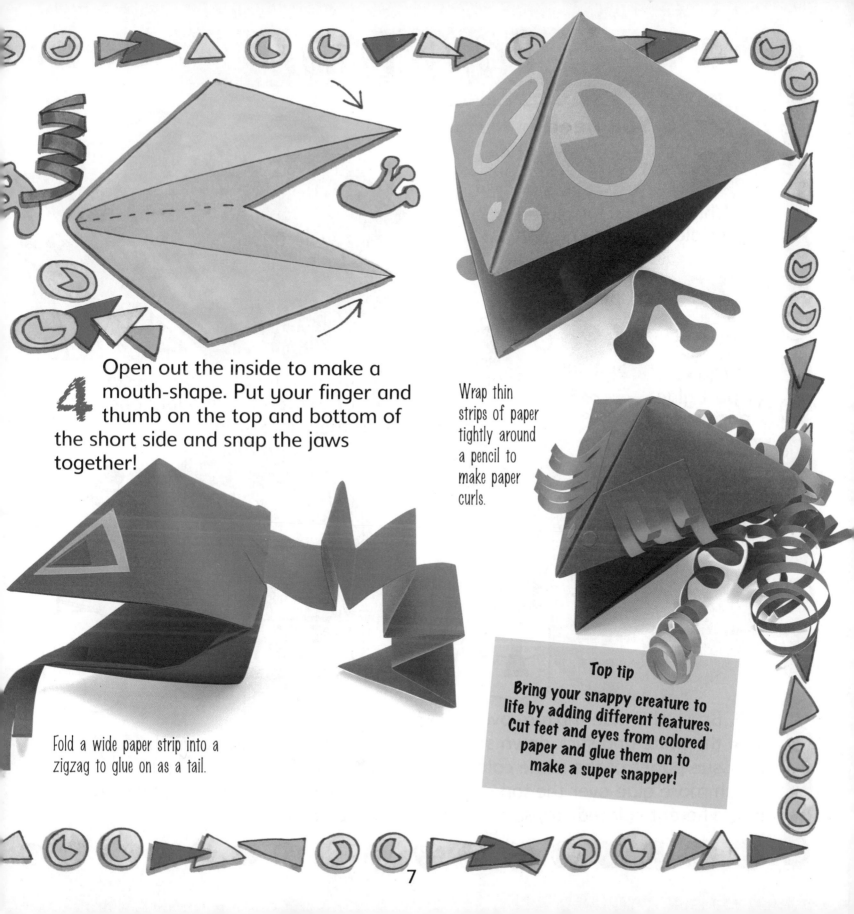

4 Open out the inside to make a mouth-shape. Put your finger and thumb on the top and bottom of the short side and snap the jaws together!

Wrap thin strips of paper tightly around a pencil to make paper curls.

Fold a wide paper strip into a zigzag to glue on as a tail.

Top tip

Bring your snappy creature to life by adding different features. Cut feet and eyes from colored paper and glue them on to make a super snapper!

7

Pretty Plates

You need

White paper plate

Colored tissue paper

Paper clip

Glue (1 part glue, 1 part water)

Sequins

Scissors

Tape

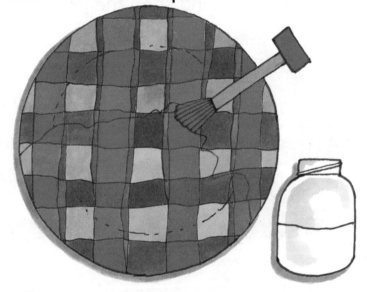

1 Choose three or four pieces of colored tissue paper and tear them into strips.

Start with the darkest tissue paper and finish with the lightest.

2 Brush the glue mixture over the plate and stick down strips of tissue paper of the same color. Brush more glue over the top and add different colored strips.

3 After sticking down the final layer leave the plate to dry thoroughly. Then add a layer of glue as a varnish.

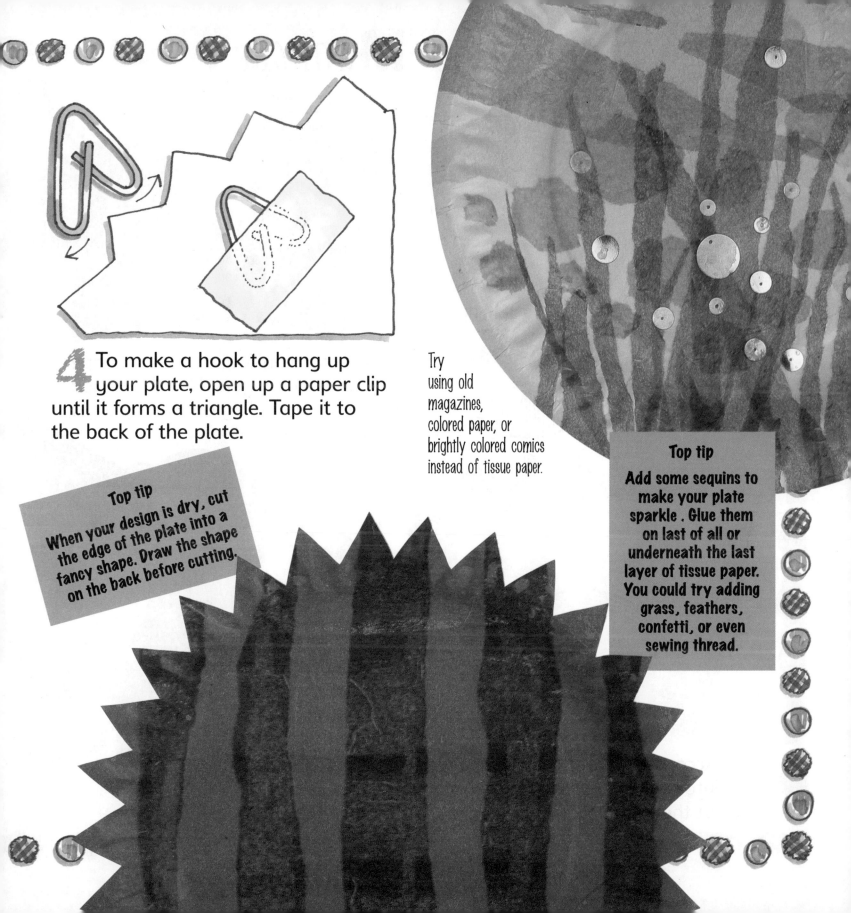

4 To make a hook to hang up your plate, open up a paper clip until it forms a triangle. Tape it to the back of the plate.

Try using old magazines, colored paper, or brightly colored comics instead of tissue paper.

Top tip

When your design is dry, cut the edge of the plate into a fancy shape. Draw the shape on the back before cutting.

Top tip

Add some sequins to make your plate sparkle . Glue them on last of all or underneath the last layer of tissue paper. You could try adding grass, feathers, confetti, or even sewing thread.

Monkey Madness

You need

Thumbtack

Pink paper

Thick brown paper

Pencil

Black felt-tip pen

Glue   Scissors

Paper clips

String

Use paper clips to hold the layers together.

1 Accordion-fold the brown paper into four layers. Use the template to draw a monkey on the top layer and cut around it.

2 Accordion-fold the pink paper into four layers. Draw two ovals and cut them out.

3 Glue an oval onto both sides of all of the monkeys' heads. Draw on a smile and eyes.

4

Make a hole through the head of one monkey with a thumbtack and tie string through the hole. Hook the other monkeys on by their arms, legs, or tails.

Trace this template and use it for your monkey shape.

Top tip
You could alternate your monkeys with another set of a different color.

Sea Scene

You need

Scissors

Glue

Thin card

Poster putty

Tissue paper

Pencil

Lining paper

1 Stick the lining paper onto a wall with poster putty. Draw a large sea scene, in pencil, with an underwater cave and a seafloor.

Choose green, blue, purple, and turquoise colors for the sea and yellow, orange, brown, and beige colors for the seabed.

2 Tear large and small shapes from different-colored tissue paper. Glue these onto the lining paper, starting at the top with the sea.

3 Draw different-shaped fish on thin card and add on three tabs. Cut around the whole shape including the tabs. Glue on bright-colored tissue or pieces of colored paper.

Top tip

To create a colorful underwater world, try making seaweed, starfish, sea horses, urchins, anemones, octopuses, and pebbles using tabs to glue them to the scene.

Try using torn magazine pictures to create the colored background.

4 Put the fish face down and fold back the tabs. Then fold each tab in half.

5 Glue the half tabs and stick them to the sea scene. Your fish will look as if it is swimming toward you!

Summer Flowers

You need

Wooden dowel

Crêpe paper

Glue

Thick card

Pencil

Tape

Scissors

1 Cut long strips from green crêpe paper. Tape one end of a strip to the wooden dowel and wind it around the dowel. Repeat until the dowel is covered.

2 Cut out a large circle from the card. Accordian-fold some yellow crêpe paper. Draw a large petal on the top fold and cut around it.

3 Glue each petal to the edge of the circle of card. Scrunch small pieces of crêpe paper and glue them on, covering the whole circle of card.

Arrange your flowers in a large, tall vase.

4 Tape the back of the flower head to the wooden dowel stem. Cut out leaf shapes from green crêpe paper and glue them to the stem.

Monster Masks

You need

Large paper bag

Colored and patterned paper

Scissors

Glue

1 Cut two eyeholes in the paper bag (see **Top tip**). Cut some colored paper into two long strips and roll them up. Put glue around the eyeholes and press the strips in place.

2 Cut two strips of paper for a toothy grin and two more strips for eyebrows. Fold them into zigzags and glue them in position.

3 Tear a nose and cheek shapes from some paper. Glue these in position.

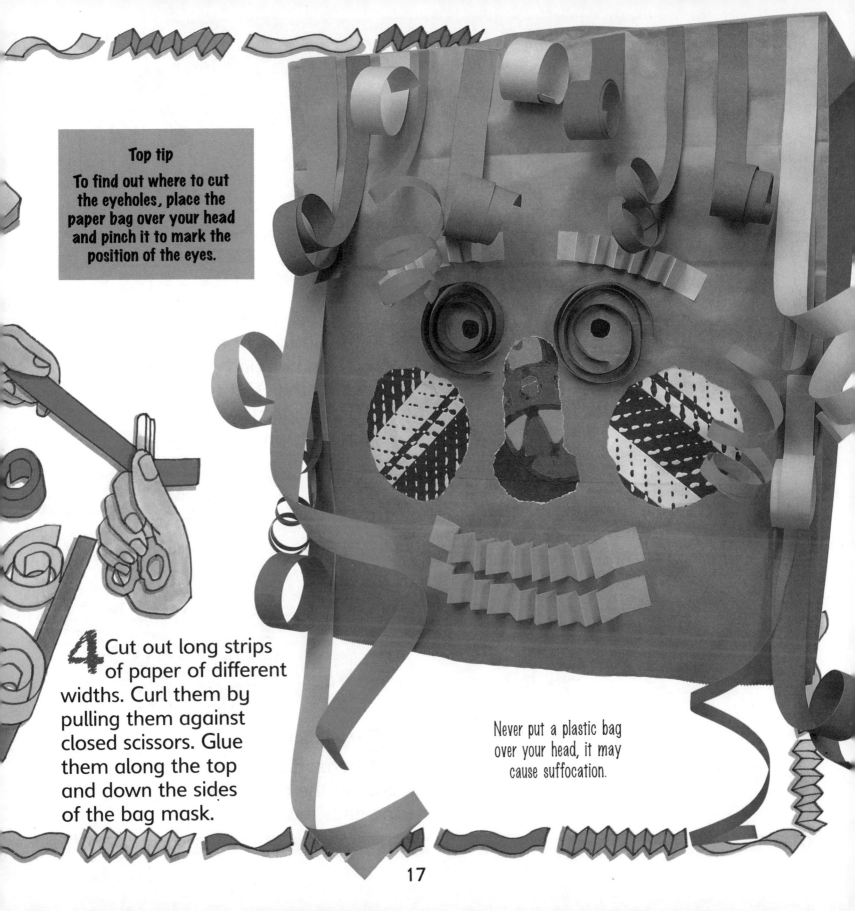

Top tip
To find out where to cut the eyeholes, place the paper bag over your head and pinch it to mark the position of the eyes.

4 Cut out long strips of paper of different widths. Curl them by pulling them against closed scissors. Glue them along the top and down the sides of the bag mask.

Never put a plastic bag over your head, it may cause suffocation.

Mini Baskets

You need

Wrapping paper

Glue

Scissors

Ruler

Pencil

Stapler

15"

2½"

8"

1 Cut a 2½-inch wide strip off the bottom of the paper. Fold the rest in half and glue the plain sides together. Cut two 15-inch x 1¼-inch wide strips and seven 8-inch x 1¼-inch wide strips.

2 Overlap one of the long strips and staple the ends. Pinch four corners to make a square. Now follow the directions to do the weaving.

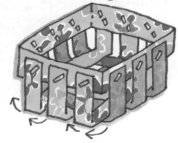

Staple three short strips to one side of the square and staple the other ends to the opposite side.

Do the same on the remaining sides of the square, weaving the second three strips through the first three.

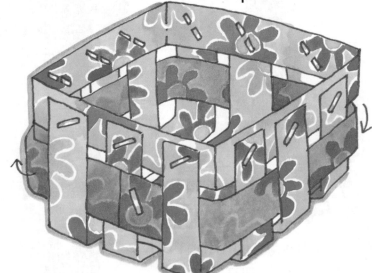

3 Weave the other long strip horizontally through the sides of the basket and staple the ends together.

4 Fold the 2½-inch wide strip in half lengthwise and slot it over the lip of the basket. Cut it to fit and staple the ends together. Staple the last short strip to two sides of the basket to make a handle.

Top tip
Line the basket with tissue paper and fill it with chocolates as a gift.

Top tip
Use colored paper or thin card in contrasting colors. You don't need to glue it together to make it double-sided. You could also paint your own pattern on thin card stock.

Mission Control

You need

1 large cardboard box

3 small boxes

Glue

Craft knife

Thin card

Tape

Toilet-paper tube

Colored cellophane

Silver foil

Bottle caps

Buttons

1 Draw diagonal lines on both ends of a small, square box. Cut along these lines to make a wedge shape. Cut a piece of box and tape it to the open side. Tape the wedge shape onto a larger box.

When the boxes are covered, tape them together.

2 Ask an adult to cut windows in the boxes. Cover all the boxes with foil and glue down the edges. Cut pieces of cellophane to fit the windows and tape them in place.

3 Cut circles from thin card and glue foil or colored cellophane onto them. Make a cut to the middle of each circle. Overlap the ends and tape them together to make a cone.

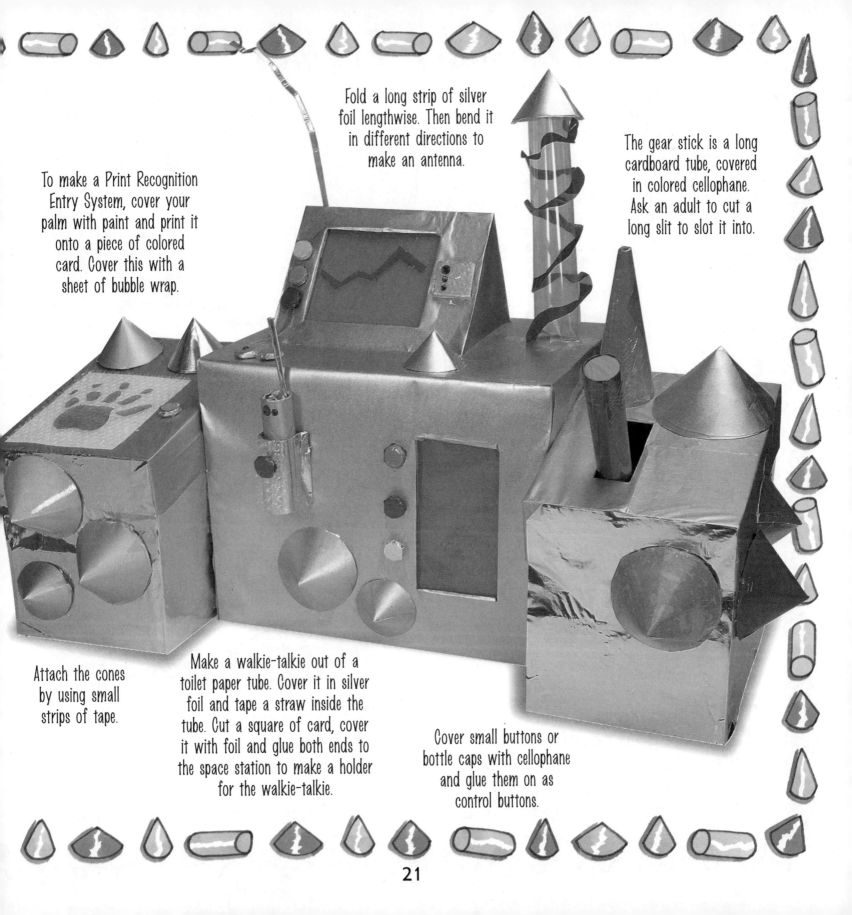

To make a Print Recognition Entry System, cover your palm with paint and print it onto a piece of colored card. Cover this with a sheet of bubble wrap.

Fold a long strip of silver foil lengthwise. Then bend it in different directions to make an antenna.

The gear stick is a long cardboard tube, covered in colored cellophane. Ask an adult to cut a long slit to slot it into.

Attach the cones by using small strips of tape.

Make a walkie-talkie out of a toilet paper tube. Cover it in silver foil and tape a straw inside the tube. Cut a square of card, cover it with foil and glue both ends to the space station to make a holder for the walkie-talkie.

Cover small buttons or bottle caps with cellophane and glue them on as control buttons.

Friendly Frames

You need

Cardboard

Gold and silver paper

Scissors

Glue

Craft knife

Pencil

Brush

Paint

1 Cut two squares of cardboard the same size. Paint one in a bright color and draw a smaller square in the center of it. Ask an adult to cut out the square with a craft knife.

Make sure you cut through all the layers of paper.

2 Cut two strips of silver paper and two of gold paper the same length as the picture frame but not quite as wide. Accordion-fold each strip. Now draw a shape on the top fold of each.

3 Cut out each shape carefully. Unfold the strips and glue them above and below the hole in the frame. Trim the ends off the other strips and glue them in the remaining spaces.

4 Spread glue onto the plain square of cardboard. Glue a picture in the middle and your decorated frame on top.

Top tip
Glue only three edges of the frame so you can change your picture by sliding in a new one.

Safari Days

You need

Colored paper

Thin card

Yarn

Darning needle

Scissors

Calendar

Glue

Pencil

Tape

1 Draw a lion's head on light orange paper and a lion's body on dark orange paper and cut them out. Then cut a large square of green paper.

Use different colored yarn to make the picture more colorful.

2 Glue the lion's head and body onto the green paper. Using a darning needle and yarn, sew a face, mane, tail, claws, and fur onto the lion (see **Sewing tip**).

3 Cut out a piece of thin card that is larger than your picture. Glue your picture onto the card. Sew around the edge of the picture with the yarn as before.

4 Make a loop from a short piece of yarn. Tape it onto the back of the picture at the top. Tape the calendar onto the back of the picture at the bottom.

Sewing tip

To sew the stitches, start by making a knot at the end of the yarn. Now push the needle through from the back of the card to the front. Pull the yarn through the hole and then push the needle through to the back in a different place. Repeat until you have finished. Finally, knot the yarn at the back.

To make the eyes, sew four stitches across each other in a star shape.

To make the nose, sew three stitches in a triangle.

1 Draw different shapes on thin card and cut them out. Roll up small pieces of paper and glue them around the edge of the card shapes to create a frame.

2 Cover the edge of the frame with thin strips of newspaper dipped in glue. When it is dry, paint the frame.

3 Glue a photo or magazine picture in the center of the frame, or paint a mini picture in the center. Spread a thin layer of glue over the top as a varnish.

EASYART
Draw

CONTENTS

Before you start working, put on old clothes or an apron so that you won't splash your good clothes with glue or paint.

Always ask an adult for help when using sharp objects such as craft knives and sharp scissors. You can buy round-ended safety scissors at most craft shops.

You can use lots of different types of glue, but a craft glue is one of the best. A glue stick is good for sticking pieces of paper together.

Remember to put the tops back on your felt-tip pens, or they will dry out.

You can use powdered paints or make shiny paint by mixing powdered paint with liquid craft glue.

28

Lead in pencils can be hard or soft. A hard pencil has **H** on the side and makes a thin, dark line. A soft pencil has **B** on the side; it makes a line which can be easily smudged with your finger or a cotton swab.

Craft shops are good places to buy all the equipment that you will need to make the things in this book.

To keep your crayon drawings and rubbings as good as new, ask an adult to spray them with hairspray from 12 inches (30 cm) away. This gives them a shiny coating.

It is a good idea to keep crayons, scrap paper, string, and other bits and pieces you have collected in a box. Then you will have them handy when you need to use them.

Pressure Drawing

You need

White paper

Colored pencils or wax crayons

Pencil

Ballpoint pen

1 Lightly sketch a picture on a piece of white paper.

2 Place this picture on top of another piece of white paper. Go over your pencil sketch with a ballpoint pen, pressing down very hard.

3 Remove the top piece of paper. Your drawing is now pressed into the piece of paper underneath.

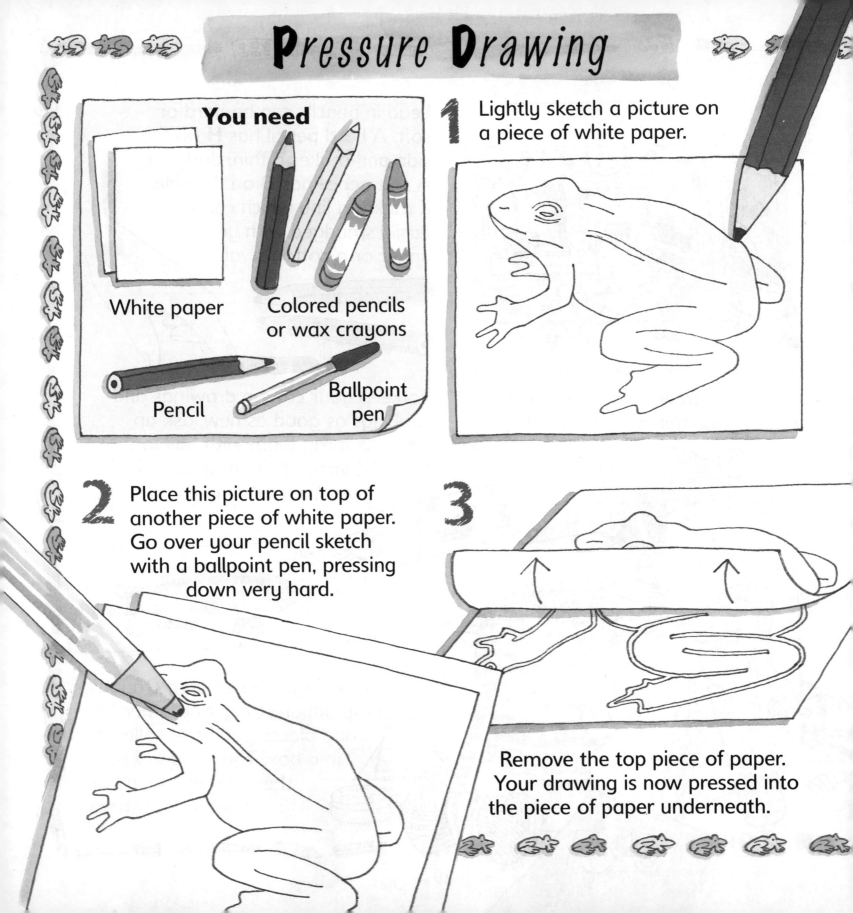

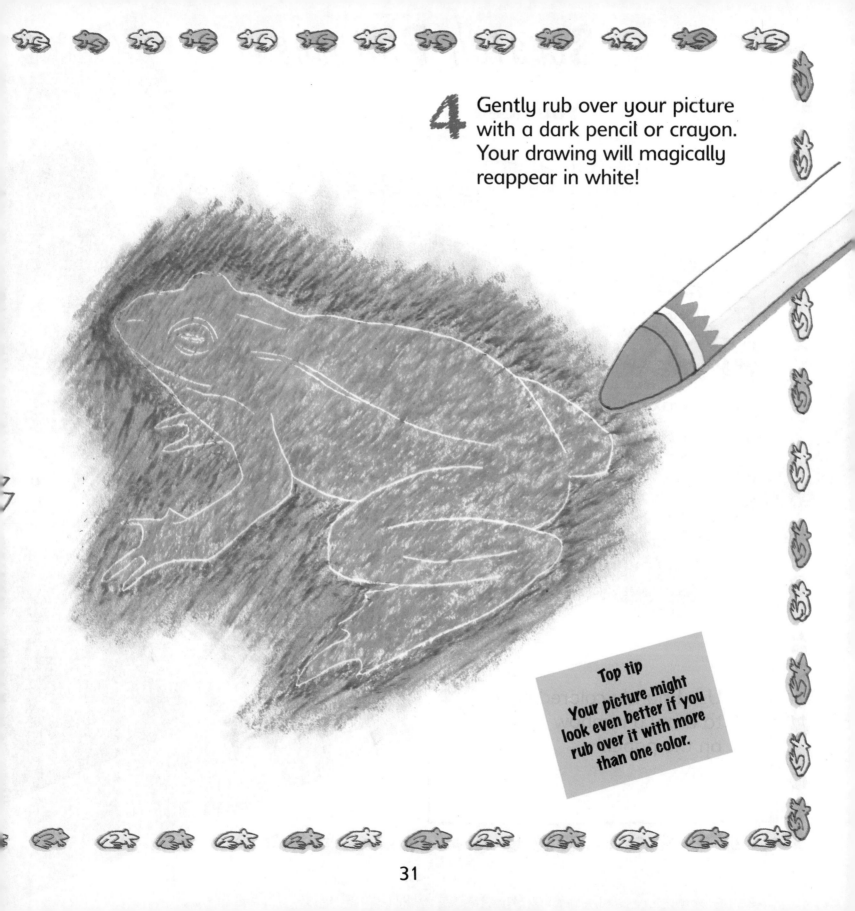

4 Gently rub over your picture with a dark pencil or crayon. Your drawing will magically reappear in white!

Top tip
Your picture might look even better if you rub over it with more than one color.

Scratch Pictures

You need

Paper

Colored pencils

Coin

Dark wax crayon

1 Use brightly colored pencils to draw a rainbow of colors on the paper.

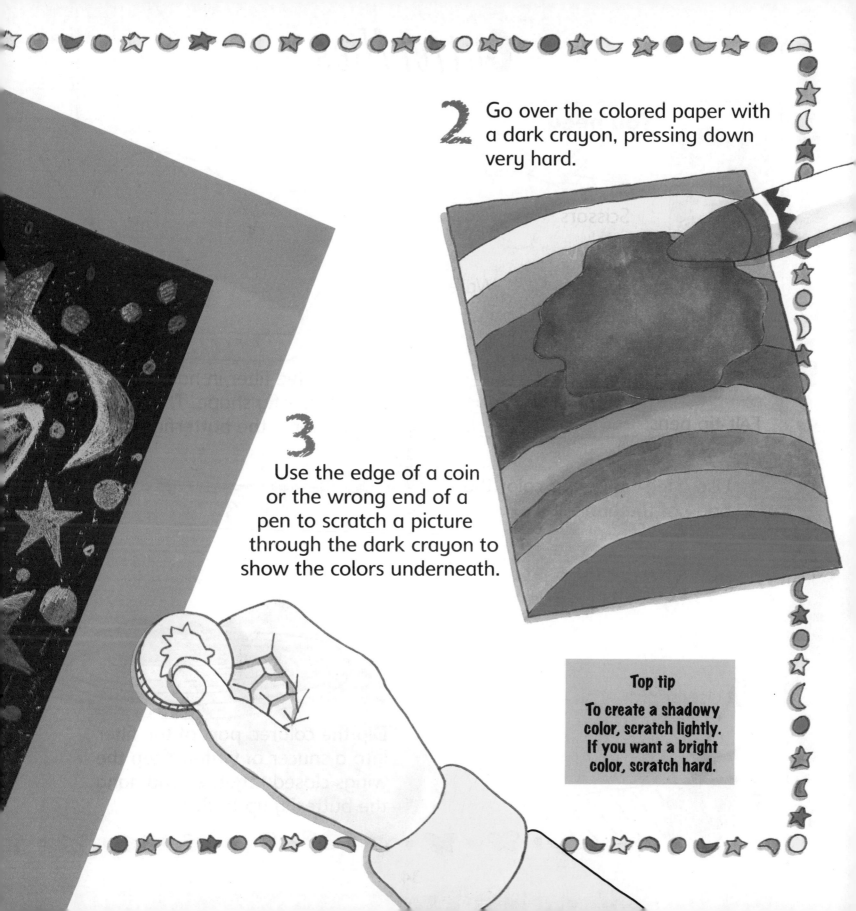

2 Go over the colored paper with a dark crayon, pressing down very hard.

3 Use the edge of a coin or the wrong end of a pen to scratch a picture through the dark crayon to show the colors underneath.

Top tip

To create a shadowy color, scratch lightly. If you want a bright color, scratch hard.

Butterflies

You need

Coffee filters

Scissors

Water

Felt-tip pens

1 Fold a coffee filter in half. Then cut out a half butterfly shape. The folded bottom of the filter is the butterfly's body.

2 Use a felt-tip pen to color the body of the butterfly.

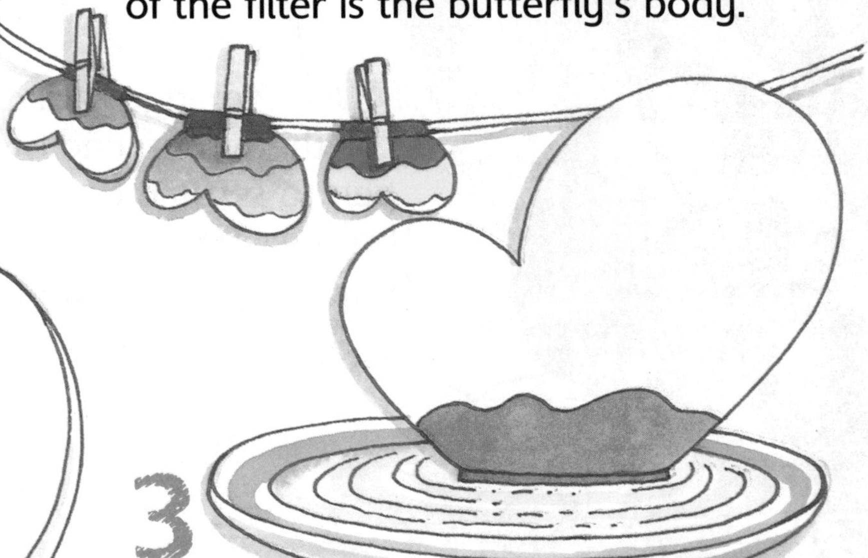

3 Dip the colored part of the filter into a saucer of water. Keep the wings closed together and hang the butterfly up to dry.

34

4

When you open up the butterfly, the color will have spread outward onto the wings. You may see more than one color!

Life-size Portraits

You need

A roll of craft paper

Scissors

Crayons

A friend

1 Roll out some plain craft paper on the floor.

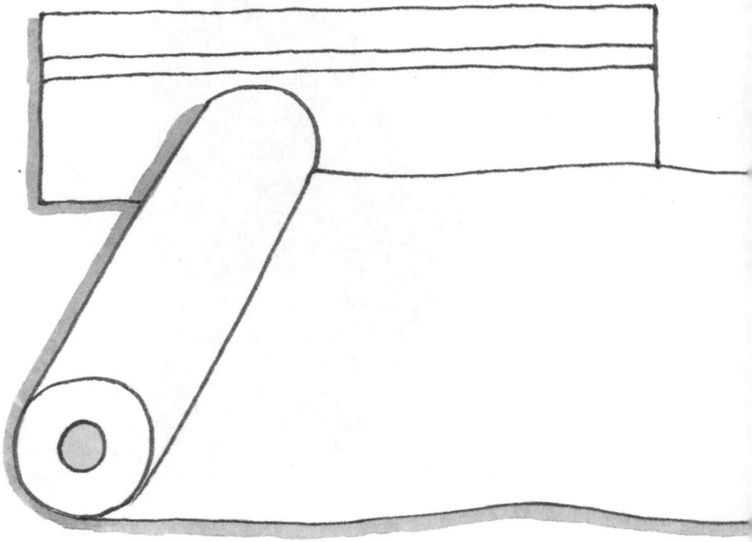

2 Ask a friend to lie down on the paper and draw around him or her.

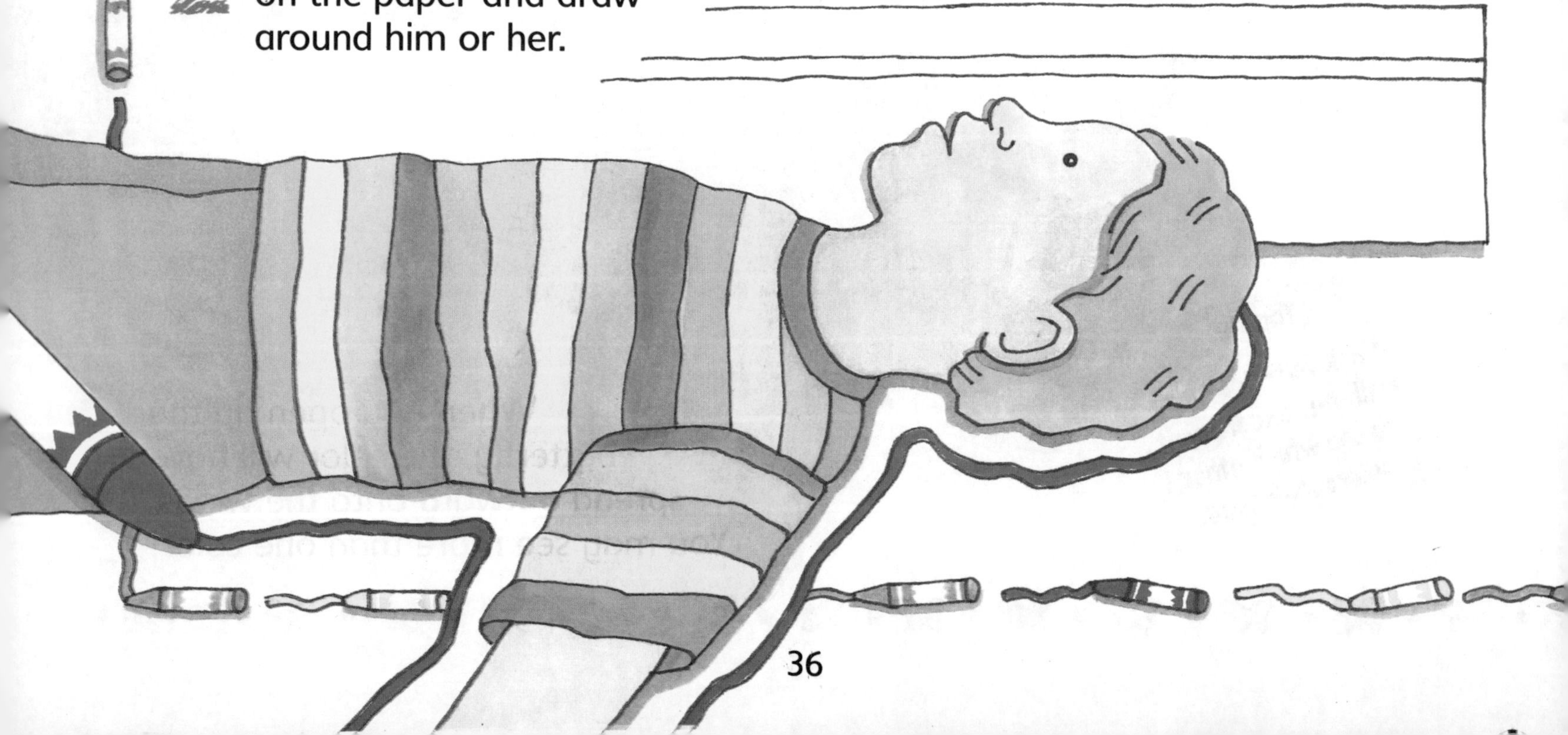

3

Color inside the outline with crayons to make a life-size portrait.

Top tip
Ask your friend to wear old clothes in case you get crayon marks on them.

Crayon Silhouettes

You need

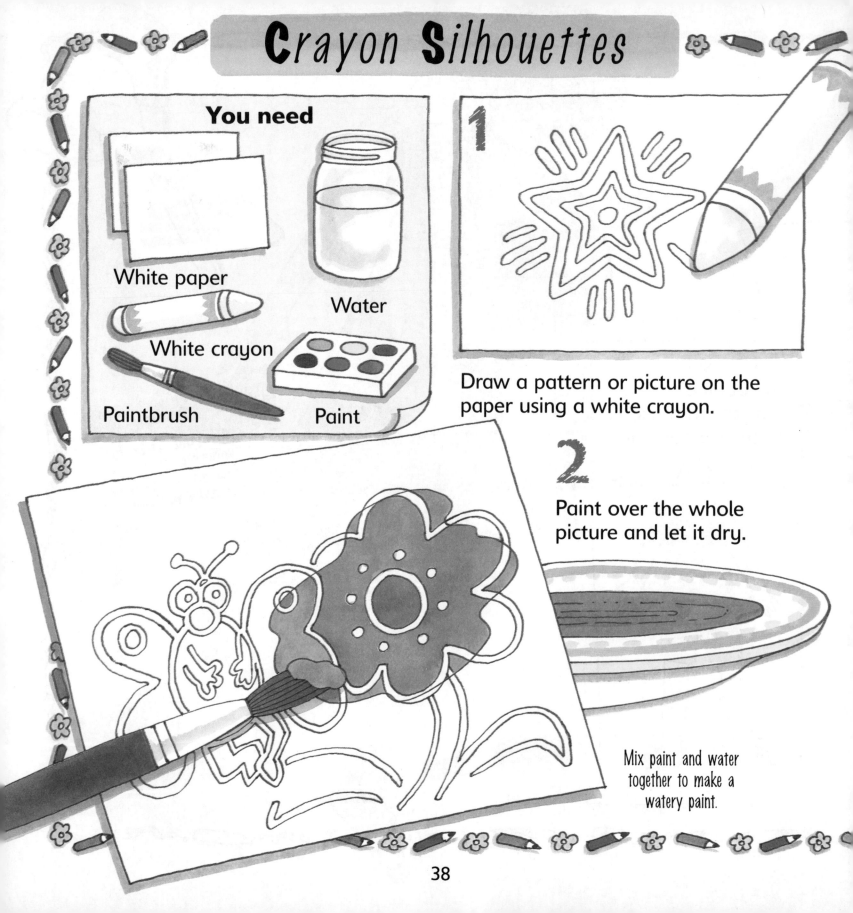

White paper

White crayon

Paintbrush

Water

Paint

1 Draw a pattern or picture on the paper using a white crayon.

2 Paint over the whole picture and let it dry.

Mix paint and water together to make a watery paint.

3
The paint will not stick to the white crayon picture.

String Drawings

You need

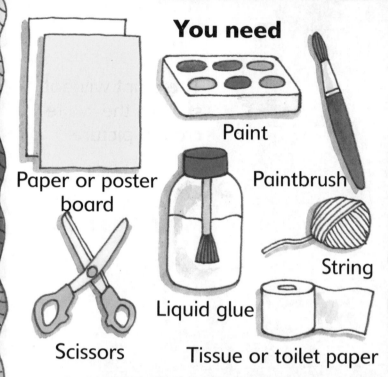

Paper or poster board

Paint

Paintbrush

String

Liquid glue

Scissors

Tissue or toilet paper

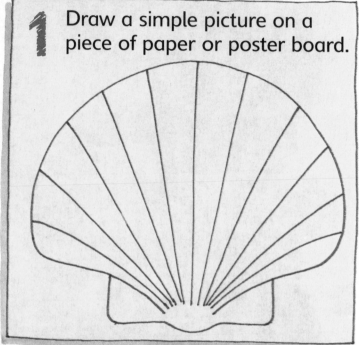

1 Draw a simple picture on a piece of paper or poster board.

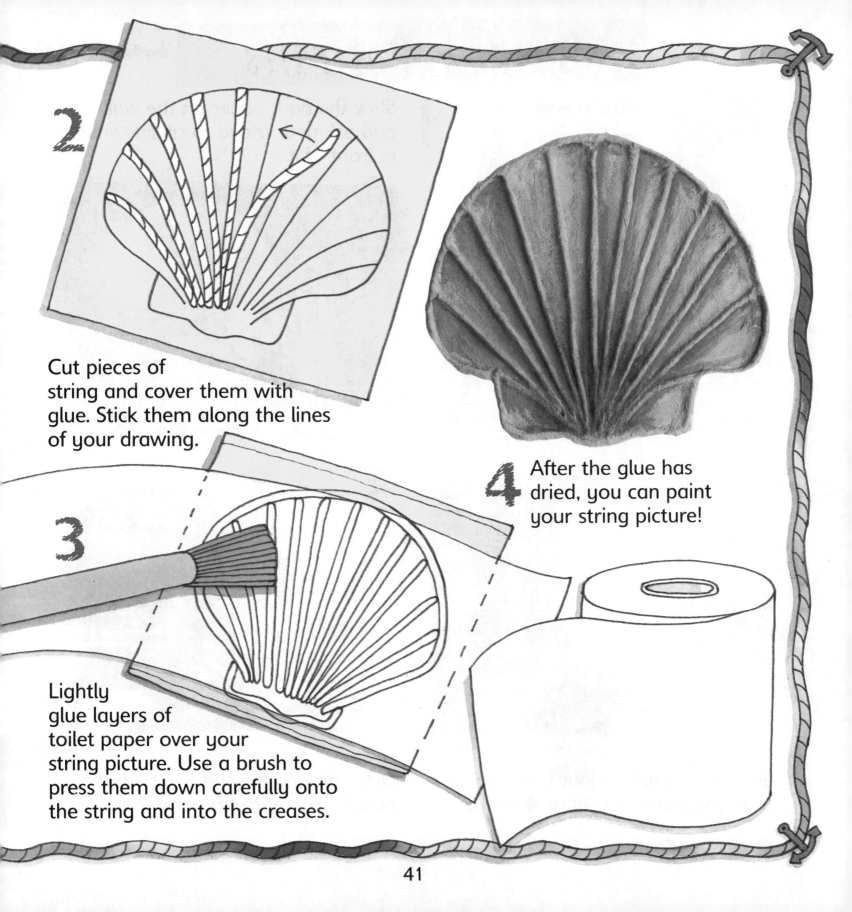

2

Cut pieces of
string and cover them with
glue. Stick them along the lines
of your drawing.

3

Lightly
glue layers of
toilet paper over your
string picture. Use a brush to
press them down carefully onto
the string and into the creases.

4 After the glue has
dried, you can paint
your string picture!

41

Shadow Portraits

You need

Dark colored paper

Scissors

White paper

Colored pencil

A friend

Tape

Desk lamp

1 Stick the dark paper on the wall and ask your friend to sit sideways in front of it.

2 Shine the lamp on your friend so that you can see a sharp shadow.

3 Draw around the shadow with the pencil. Try not to press too hard.

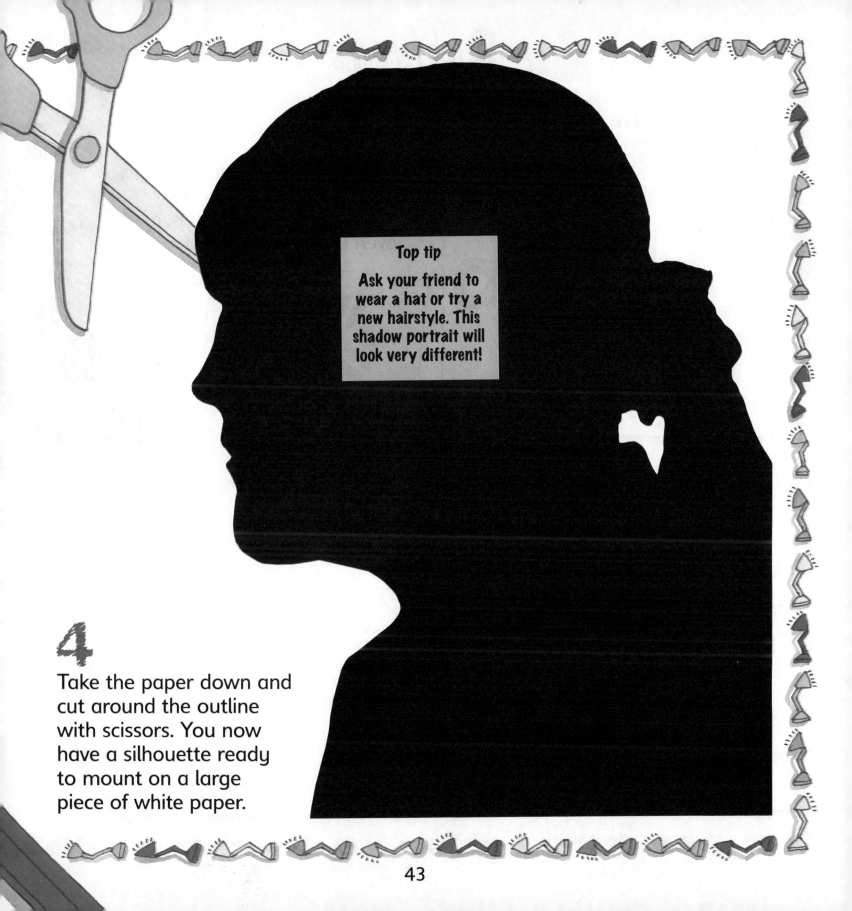

Top tip

Ask your friend to wear a hat or try a new hairstyle. This shadow portrait will look very different!

4

Take the paper down and cut around the outline with scissors. You now have a silhouette ready to mount on a large piece of white paper.

Rubbings

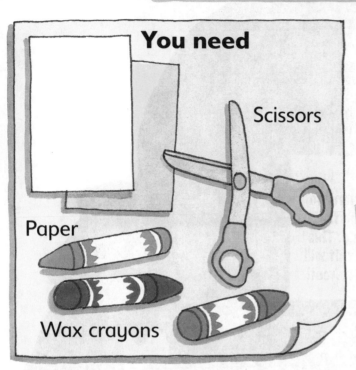

You need

Scissors

Paper

Wax crayons

2

Make lots of different patterns. You can try rubbing over bricks, bicycle tires, coins, or even the sole of your shoe!

1 Lay paper over a rough surface such as a piece of tree bark and rub a crayon over it.
A pattern will appear!

3

Cut out shapes from your rubbings and make a picture with them. Stick them on colored paper or a larger rubbing.

Top tip
Remember that the knobbier the surface, the better your rubbing will be.

Foil Frames

You need

Craft foil

Ballpoint pen

Ink

Scissors or craft knife

String

Glue

Cereal box

Tape

2 Pressing firmly with the ballpoint pen, draw shapes and patterns on the foil frame.

1 Choose a picture and cut a foil frame 2 inches (5cm) bigger than your picture. Cut a hole in the middle which is smaller than your picture.

Ask an adult to cut out the frame for you.

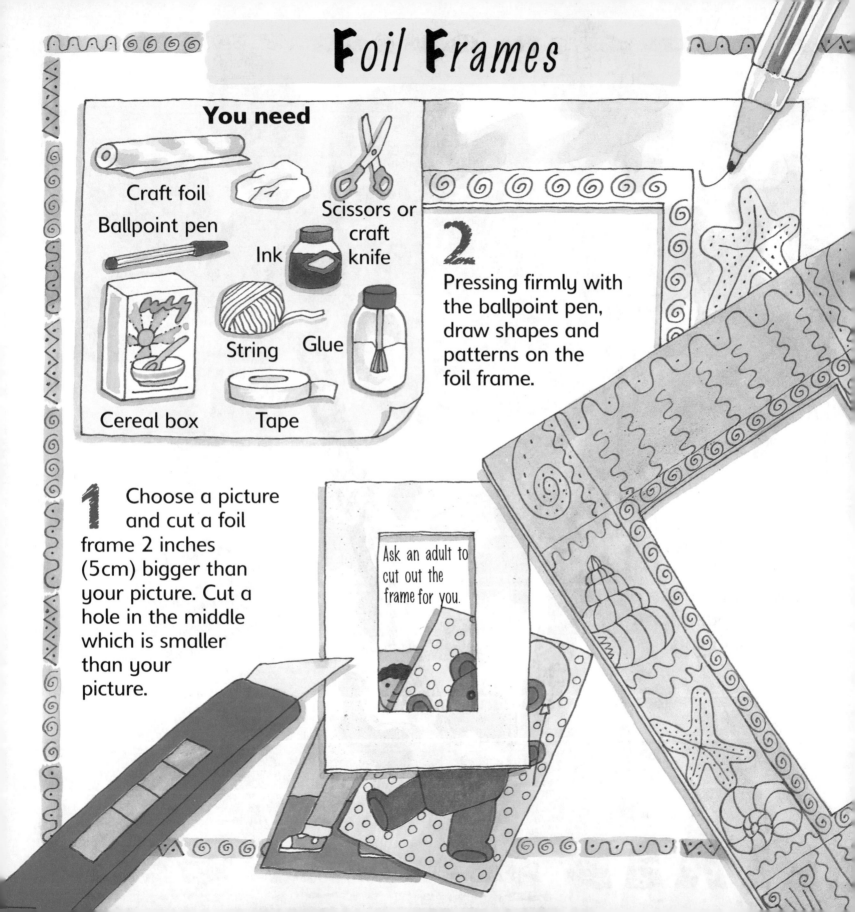

4

Cut a piece of cardboard from the cereal box. Make it the same size as your frame. Stick your picture in the middle of it. Now glue your foil frame in position.

Attach a loop of string to the back with tape to hang your framed picture.

3 Turn your frame over and rub a layer of ink on it. Before it dries, remove some of the ink by wiping a tissue in one direction across the frame.

More Ideas

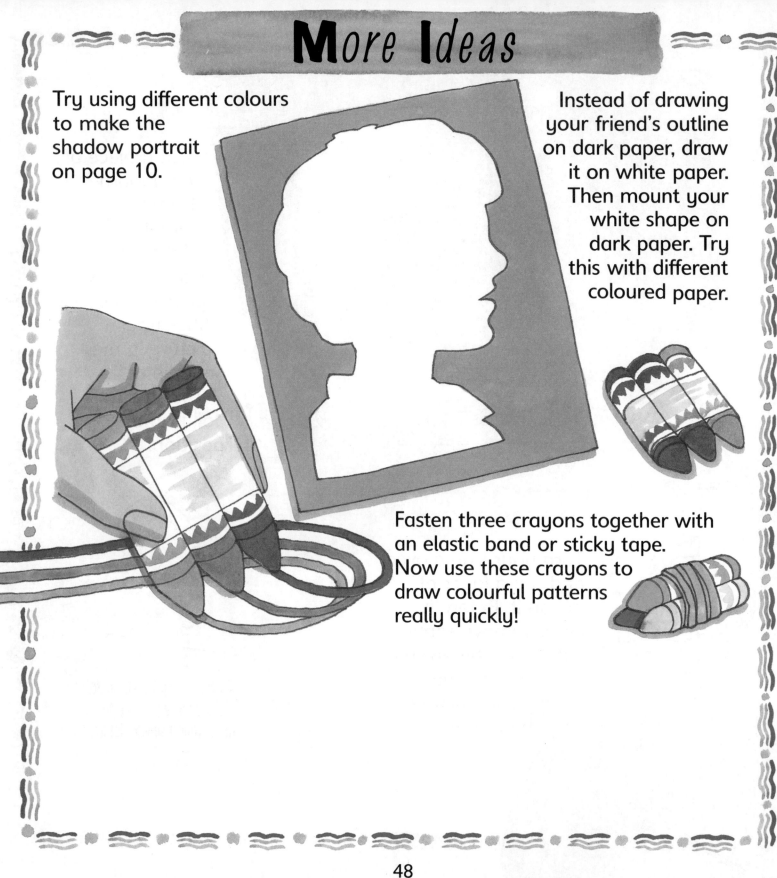

Try using different colours to make the shadow portrait on page 10.

Instead of drawing your friend's outline on dark paper, draw it on white paper. Then mount your white shape on dark paper. Try this with different coloured paper.

Fasten three crayons together with an elastic band or sticky tape. Now use these crayons to draw colourful patterns really quickly!

EasyART Stencil

CONTENTS

Hints and Tips

Collect odds and ends that can be used for stencils: jelly jars, leaves, string, doilies, old pens, magazines, and scrap paper.

There are many different types of brushes you can use to apply paint. Old toothbrushes and nailbrushes create exciting effects.

Always ask an adult for help when you need to use a craft knife. You can buy round-ended safety scissors from most craft shops.

Try using cardboard from old birthday cards, cereal boxes, and shoeboxes to make your stencils.

Use only small amounts of glue to stick things together. Too much will ruin your picture.

Cover your work area with plenty of newspaper. Stenciling can be very messy! Always remember to clean up afterward.

Be imaginative! Don't just use paints for your stencil ideas. Use pens, glitter, and scrunched-up tissue paper as well.

Put on an apron or old clothes before you start stenciling. This will protect your clothes from splashes of paint.

Glitter Fish

You need

Glitter

Poster board

Glue

Pencil

Craft knife

Thick paper

Draw a fish in segments on the poster board. Carefully cut out the segments. The piece with holes in, is your stencil. Ask an adult to help.

2 Place the stencil on some thick paper. Brush the glue over the stencil.

Top tip

Use a different color of glitter in each segment for a sparkling fish!

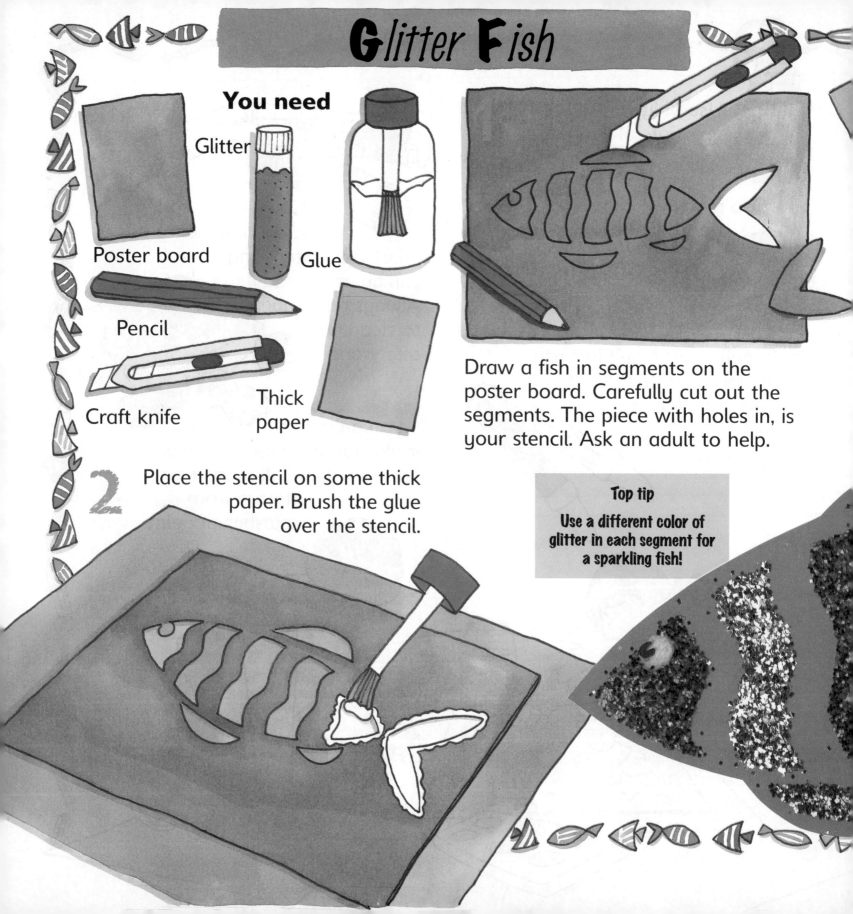

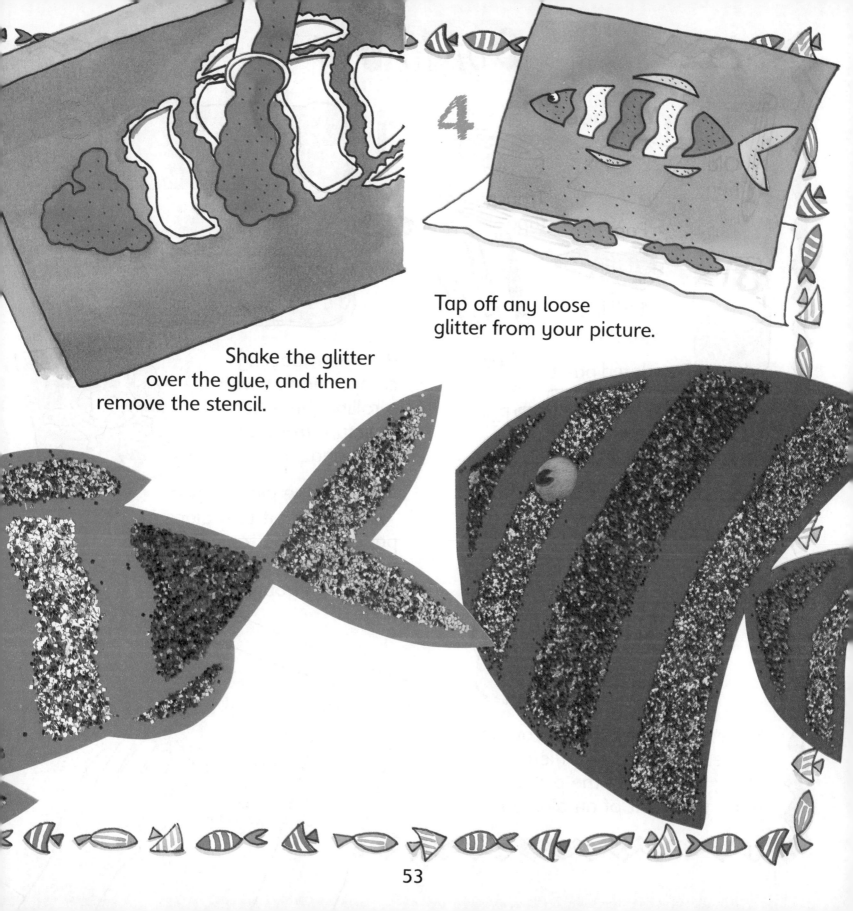

Shake the glitter over the glue, and then remove the stencil.

4 Tap off any loose glitter from your picture.

Dot to Dot

You need

Old pen

Paper

Transparent tape

Modeling compound

Powdered paint

Colored pencils

Rolling pin

1 Roll the modeling compound flat with a rolling pin. Choose a picture from an old magazine.

2 Place the picture face up over the modeling compound. Pierce holes along the lines of the picture using the point of an old pen.

3 Turn the picture over and stick it to a piece of paper with the tape. Press the powdered paint into the holes with your fingers.

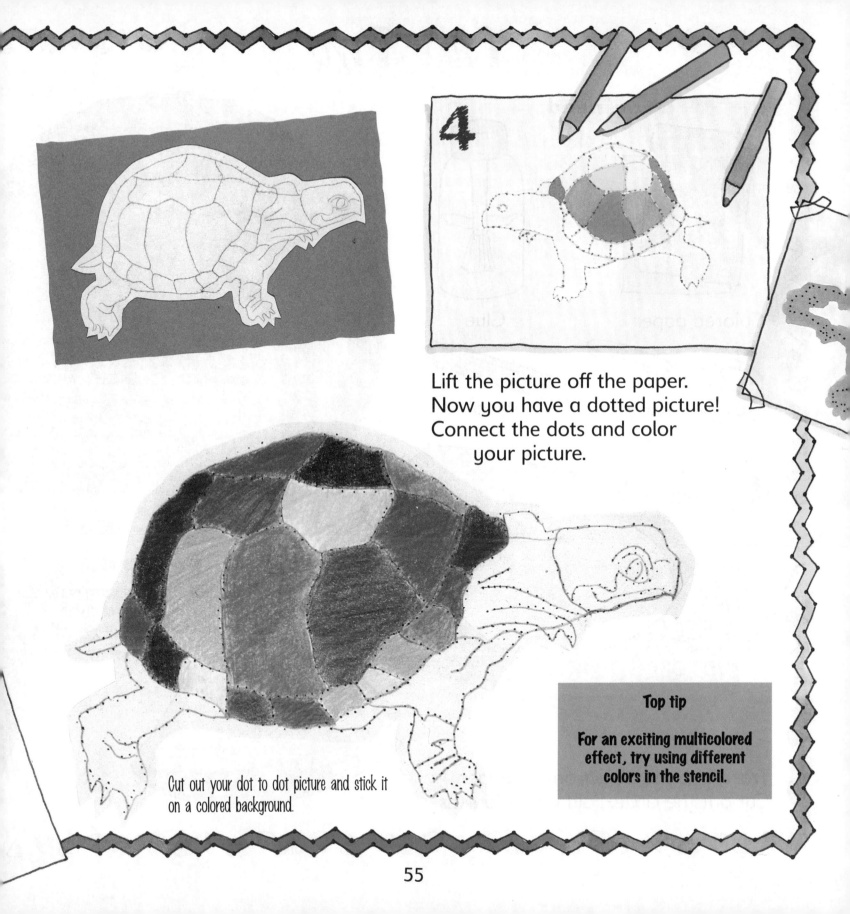

4

Lift the picture off the paper.
Now you have a dotted picture!
Connect the dots and color
your picture.

Cut out your dot to dot picture and stick it
on a colored background.

Top tip

For an exciting multicolored
effect, try using different
colors in the stencil.

Take Two

You need

Colored paper

Glue

Scissors

Pencil

1

Trace a round object on the paper.
Cut out the circle. Fold it into fourths.

Top tip

Make more amazing patterns
by gluing lots of different
stencils on top of each other.

2

Be careful not to cut all the way across the paper.

Using a pair of scissors, carefully cut shapes into the folds of the paper.

3

Unfold the paper carefully and you will have a stencil pattern. Glue it onto a piece of different colored paper to make a design.

Splattering

You need

Poster board

Powdered paints

Pencil

Craft knife

Water

Thick paper

Brush

1 Draw a picture on the poster board and cut it out. Place the poster board on top of the paper.

2 Mix the powdered paint with water, making sure that the paint is very watery.

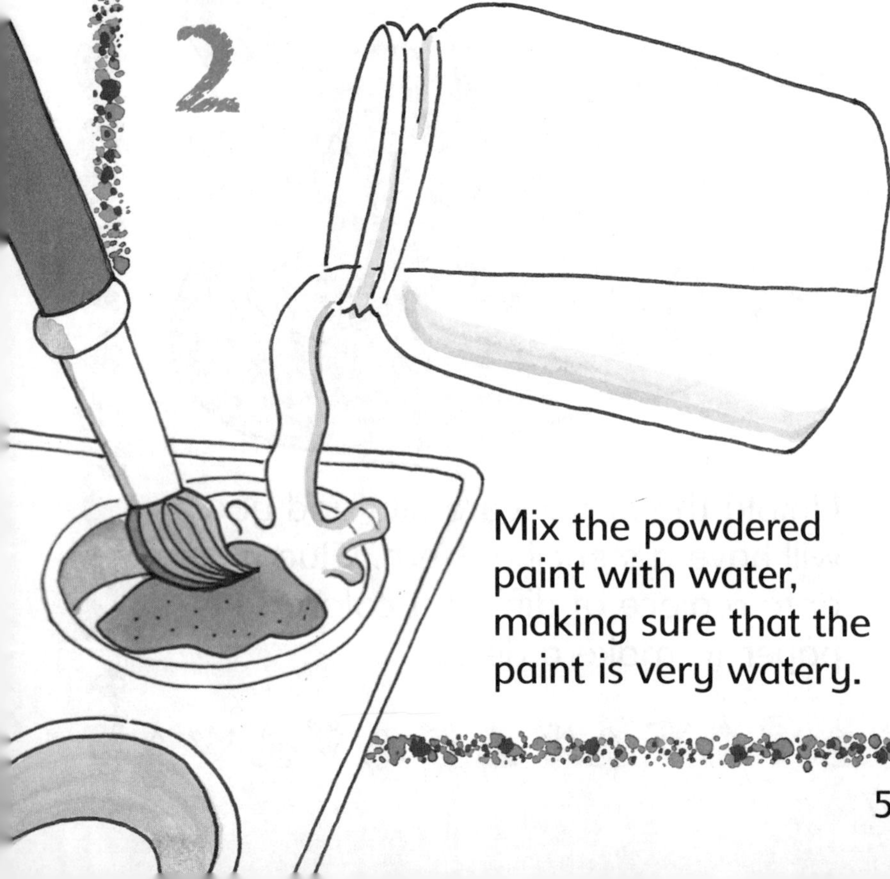

3 Dip the paintbrush into paint and splatter paint over the stencil by quickly flicking your wrist.

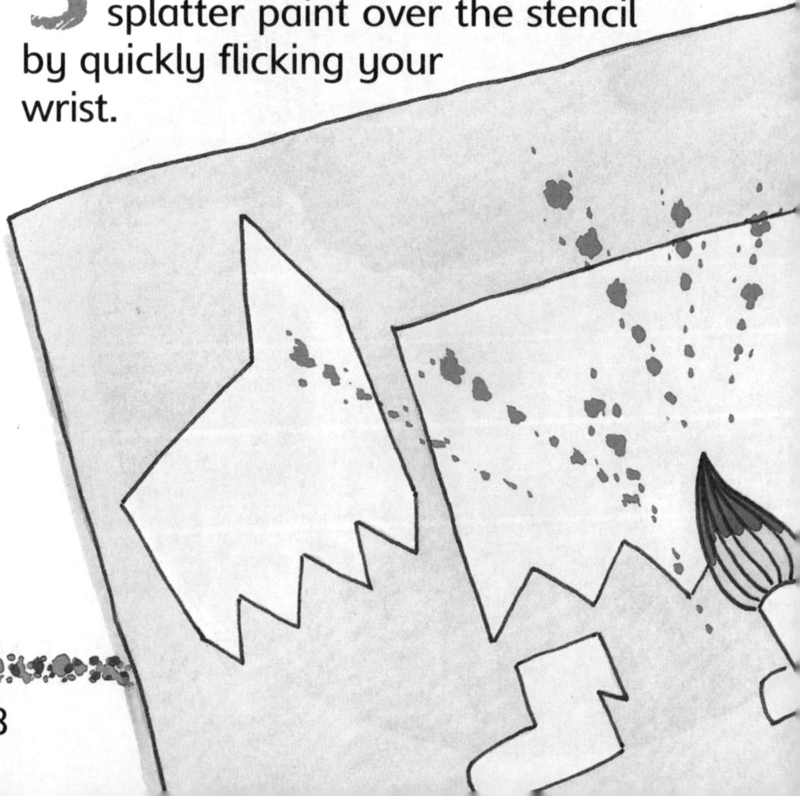

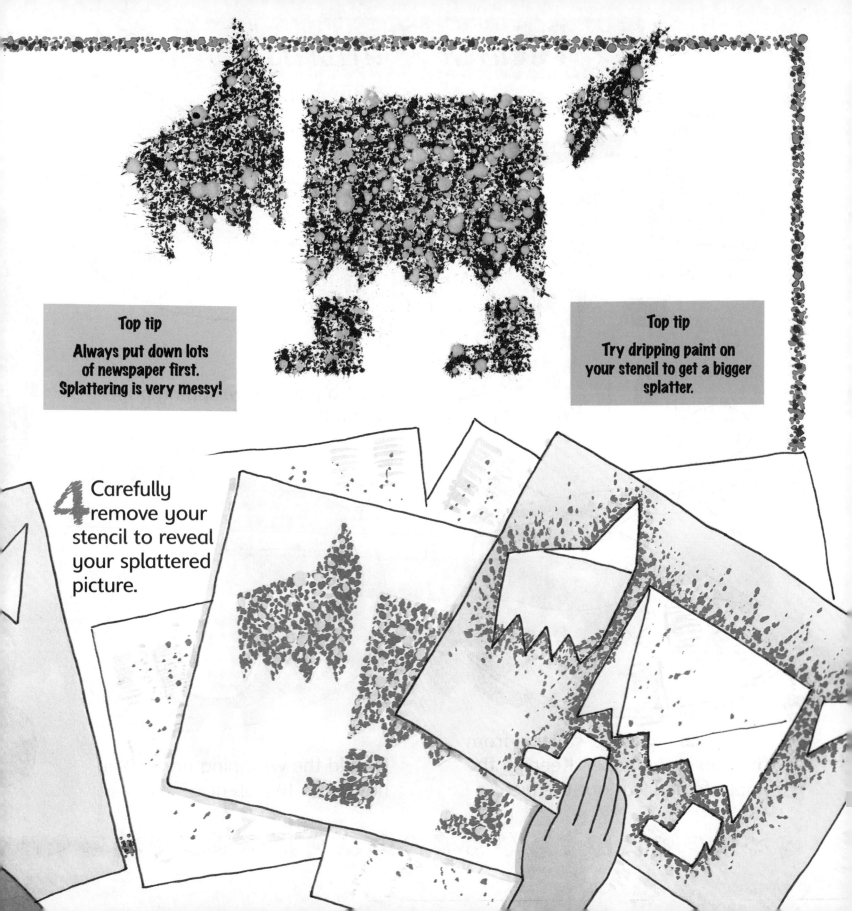

Top tip

Always put down lots of newspaper first. Splattering is very messy!

Top tip

Try dripping paint on your stencil to get a bigger splatter.

4 Carefully remove your stencil to reveal your splattered picture.

Mirror Patterns

You need

Pencil

Scissors

Colored paper

Glue

Wrapping paper

1

Take a piece of wrapping paper and fold it in half.

2

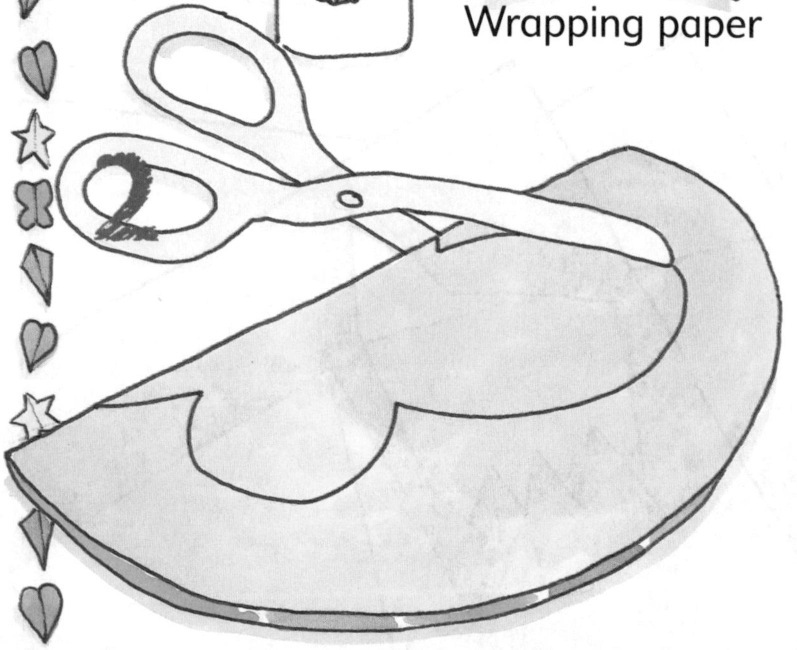

Draw half a picture, starting from the fold in the paper. Keeping the paper folded, cut out the picture.

3

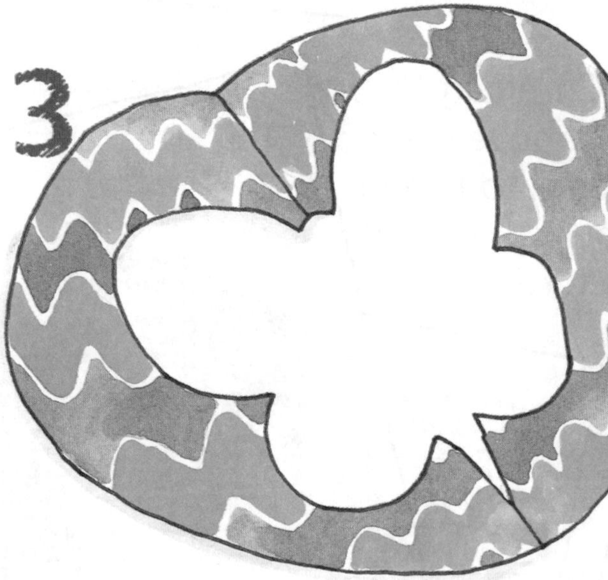

Unfold the wrapping paper. You now have two stencils.

Top tip
Glue the stencils onto colored paper to make interesting designs.

Spray Stencils

You need

Spray bottle

Powdered paint

Water

Dishwashing liquid

Poster board

Thick paper

Pencil

Scissors

Toothbrush

Craft knife

1 Cut an animal shape from the poster board with a pair of scissors. Lay the animal-shaped pieces on paper.

2 Mix the paint with water and add a little dishwashing liquid. Put the mixture into the spray bottle.

3 Shake the bottle well and spray the paint mixture over the stencil. Wait for the stencil to dry before you remove it.

Be careful not to overload your toothbrush with paint, or it will drip on your stencil.

For a different look, draw a picture on poster board. Ask an adult to cut it out with a craft knife. Lay the poster board on paper. Dip the toothbrush into paint and flick the paint over the stencil.

Use as many pieces of poster board as you want to make your design.

Printed Paper

You need

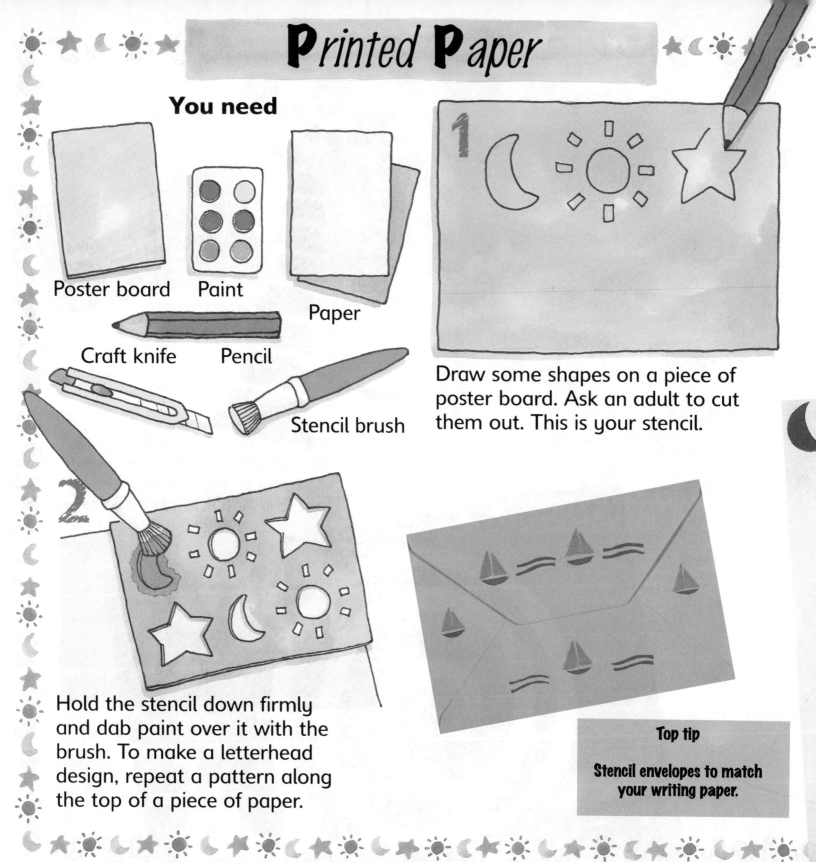

Poster board Paint

Paper

Craft knife Pencil

Stencil brush

1 Draw some shapes on a piece of poster board. Ask an adult to cut them out. This is your stencil.

2 Hold the stencil down firmly and dab paint over it with the brush. To make a letterhead design, repeat a pattern along the top of a piece of paper.

Top tip

Stencil envelopes to match your writing paper.

64

Dab paint on some string to match your wrapping paper.

Dear Jason

Thank you for my lovely birthday present. It is such fun!

Love from Ruth xx

3 To make wrapping paper, cover a large sheet of paper with a repeating pattern.

Torn Paper

You need

Paint

Paper

Brush or sponge

Water

1

Tear a piece of paper in half to make a zigzag shape.

2 Lay one half of the torn paper on top of a piece of colored paper.

Try using your torn paper to make a picture.

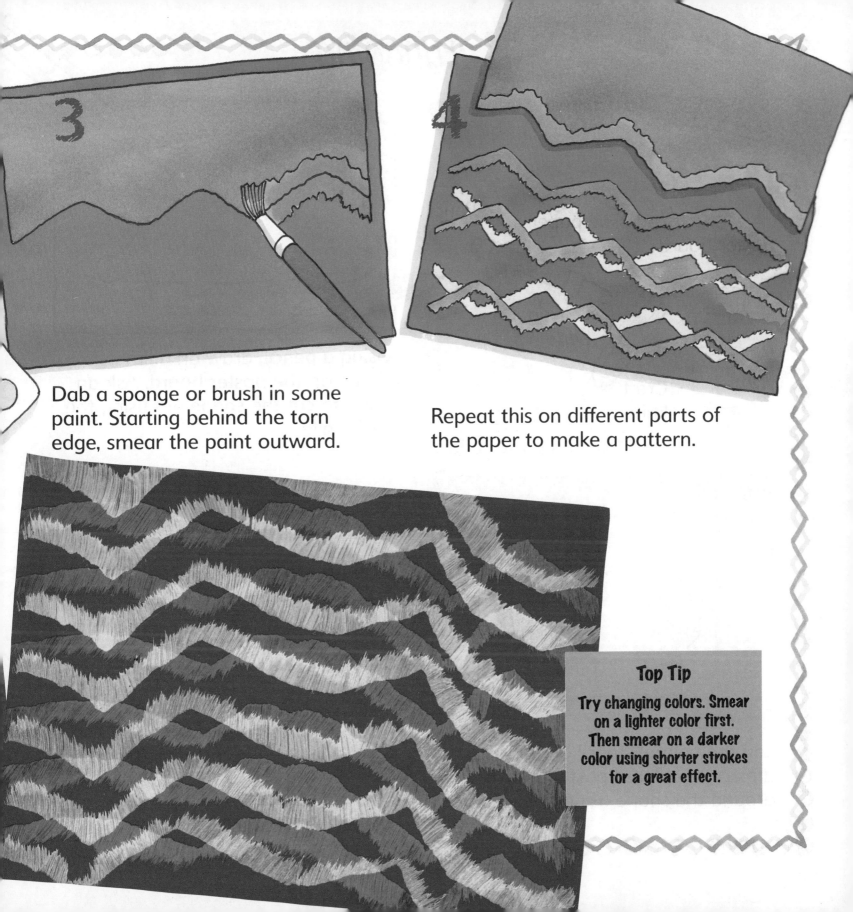

3

Dab a sponge or brush in some paint. Starting behind the torn edge, smear the paint outward.

4

Repeat this on different parts of the paper to make a pattern.

Top Tip

Try changing colors. Smear on a lighter color first. Then smear on a darker color using shorter strokes for a great effect.

Scrunching

You need

Poster board

Tissue paper

Pencil

Glue

Craft knife

Felt-tip pen

Colored poster board

1 Using a pencil, draw an animal shape on the poster board. Ask an adult to cut the shape out using the craft knife.

2 Lay the animal stencil on top of a piece of colored poster board. Draw around the shape using a felt-tip pen.

3 Tear the different colors of tissue paper into squares and scrunch them up.

69

Top tip
Put your animal in grass. Cut a jagged edge out of green poster board and stick it to the bottom of your picture.

4

Glue the colored tissue paper inside the animal shape.

Underwater

You need

Poster board   Paints   Paper

Stencil brush

Pencil

Craft knife

Water

1 Draw underwater creatures and plants on a piece of poster board.

2 Ask an adult to cut them out with a craft knife. This makes your stencil.

3 Dip the brush into paint. Press the stencil firmly down on to a sheet of paper and dab the brush on top of it.

Top tip

Keep a stencil in place using removable tape.

4

Lift the stencil off the paper and you will see your shape. Now keep stenciling creatures and plants until you have a picture.

More Ideas

Try making a spray picture like the pictures on page 15. This time use a nailbrush to flick the paint.

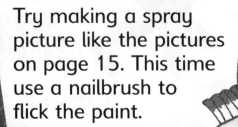

Keep moving the card shapes and use different colors of paint to build up a layered effect.

Use the stencils you made on page 13 to make pictures with repeated designs. This can also make exciting wrapping paper!

Try making gift tags to match!

EasyART
Build

CONTENTS

Hints and Tips

You can make models out of all sorts of things. Look for useful pieces of card, boxes, tubes, fabric scraps, and sticks, and save them, ready for your next idea.

Craft stores are good places to look for bits and pieces for making models. You'll find lots of new ideas there, too!

You can buy bright colored paper and cellophane from craft and stationery stores.

You can use most types of glue for making the ideas in this book. Craft glue is good for sticking paper and card. Hot glue or wood glue is best for securing uneven surfaces such as wood or plastic.

Look for modeling material, like clay and soft dough, in toy stores.

Always ask an adult for help when you are using sharp objects such as craft knives and pointed scissors.

It is a good idea to put on old clothes before you start your model-making. It can be a bit messy!

Always cover your work surface with plenty of newspaper before you start in case anything spills.

Remember to wash your paintbrushes as soon as you have finished painting.

Make sure you let the paint and glue dry thoroughly before you play with your model.

Don't forget to clean up when you have finished!

Cartoon Faces

You need

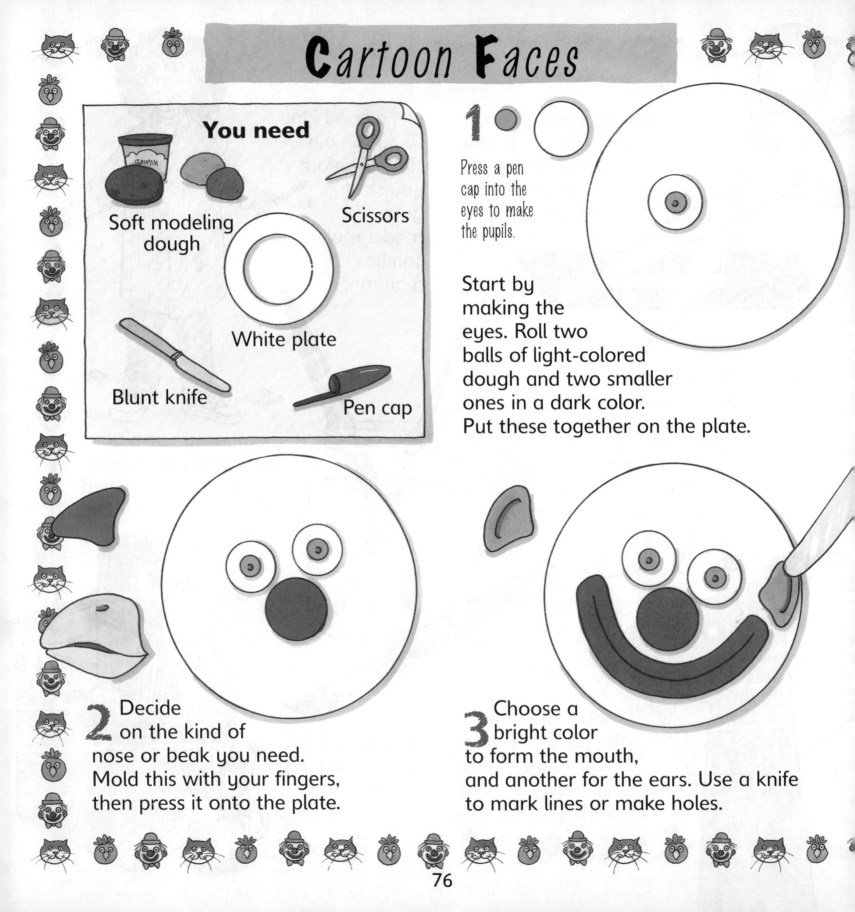

Soft modeling dough

Scissors

White plate

Blunt knife

Pen cap

1 Press a pen cap into the eyes to make the pupils.

Start by making the eyes. Roll two balls of light-colored dough and two smaller ones in a dark color. Put these together on the plate.

2 Decide on the kind of nose or beak you need. Mold this with your fingers, then press it onto the plate.

3 Choose a bright color to form the mouth, and another for the ears. Use a knife to mark lines or make holes.

4 Roll dough for hair or whiskers in spaghetti-like strands. Make feather shapes or snip into the dough to add detail.

Try making different eyes, ears, and noses to change the expression of your cartoon face.

5 Form a hat and a tie. Add little balls of dough for spots. Now arrange all the features on the plate to make your cartoon face!

Top tip

Keep your soft dough colors clear and bright by storing them in separate containers.

On Safari

You need

Craft knife

Cardboard

Poster paints

Brush

Pencil

1 Draw animal body shapes on cardboard. Ask an adult to help you cut around them with a craft knife.

2 Make two leg pieces for each animal. Cut a slot halfway down, a little narrower than the thickness of the cardboard.

3 Paint the bodies and legs on both sides, and allow them to dry. Then slot the legs on to make the animals 3-D.

So the colors don't get smudged, paint one side of each animal and allow it to dry before you paint the other side.

4 Make tree and bush shapes from cardboard. Cut a slot in the bottom edge of each shape. To stand them up, cut another shape with a slot in the top and connect the pieces slot to slot.

To make little birds sit in the trees, cut a little slot and push them on.

79

Classic Cars

You need

Paper

Paint

Strong glue

Brush

Scissors

Straws

Ruler

Rubber bands

Small box

Paper

Thick card

Ask an adult to help you make the holes.

1 Using a cup as a guide, draw four circles on thick card and cut out. Make a hole in the center of each circle, large enough to push a straw through.

2 Glue the box closed first.

Ask an adult to help you cut a hole in the top of the box for a driver's seat. Make two holes in exactly the same place on each side of the box, the size of the straws.

3 Cut three strips of thick card, twice the depth of the car. Make two slits behind the driver's seat. Push two card strips into the slits and glue one strip on top.

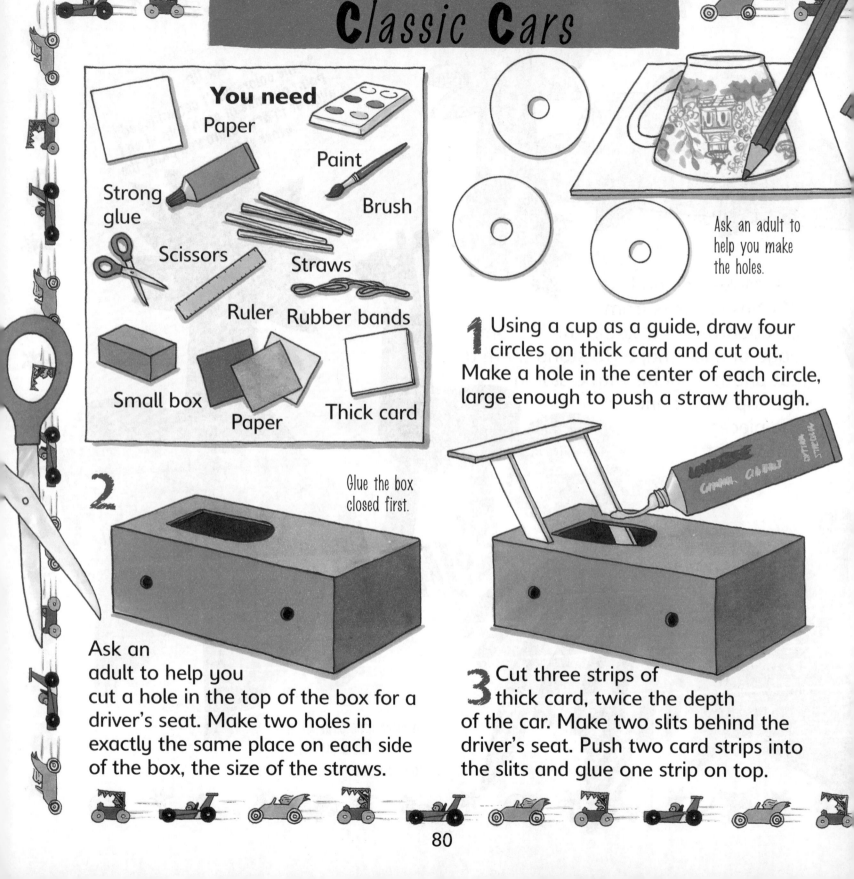

Top tip

Make sure the holes in the wheels are just big enough so that they spin freely on the straws.

4 Paint the car body and let it dry. Push two straws through the holes in either side of the car. Glue these in place on either side.

5 Push the wheels onto the straws and trim the ends off, leaving 3/8" sticking out. Wind rubber bands around to hold the wheels on. Now you're ready to go, go, go!

Bend a strip of thick card to make the driver's seat.

Cut out and glue on paper shapes for headlights, bumpers, and racing stripes.

Log Cabin

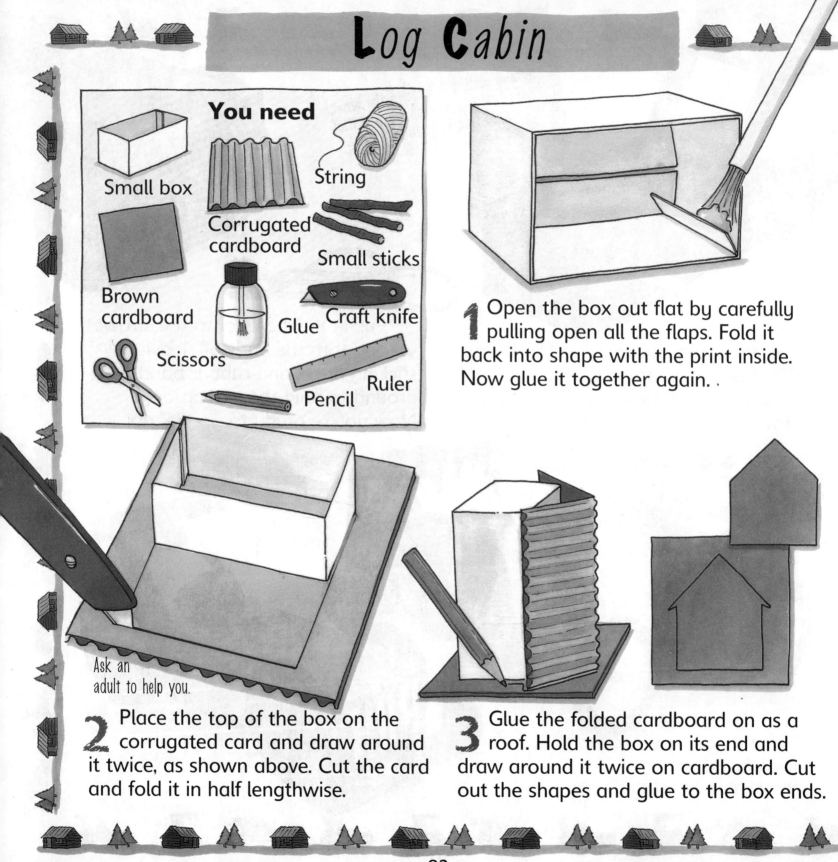

You need

Small box

Corrugated cardboard

String

Small sticks

Brown cardboard

Glue

Craft knife

Scissors

Ruler

Pencil

1 Open the box out flat by carefully pulling open all the flaps. Fold it back into shape with the print inside. Now glue it together again.

Ask an adult to help you.

2 Place the top of the box on the corrugated card and draw around it twice, as shown above. Cut the card and fold it in half lengthwise.

3 Glue the folded cardboard on as a roof. Hold the box on its end and draw around it twice on cardboard. Cut out the shapes and glue to the box ends.

4 Cut a small square and a rectangle from brown cardboard and glue on as the door and window. Now cut pieces of string to glue on as the detail.

5 Break the sticks into the right lengths and glue them to the box to complete your log cabin.

Find a little piece of fabric to make the curtains.

Top tip

Glue some green felt onto some cardboard to make a grassy base to put your model on.

Monster Munch

You need

Vegetables

Fruit

Cutting board

Knife

Spoon

Toothpicks

1 Choose a large vegetable or fruit for the body and head of the monster. Cut a hole for the mouth and scoop out the flesh.

2 Use strong root vegetables (potatoes, carrots turnips) for legs. Push toothpicks into the body and push legs onto them. Make sure your monster will balance!

3 Cut different shapes to make monster features, such as a tongue, teeth, hair, hands, and feet.

4 Break toothpicks into short lengths and push these into the body. Push the features onto these.

Use garden peas for freckles! Push them onto small pieces of toothpick.

Fantastic Fort

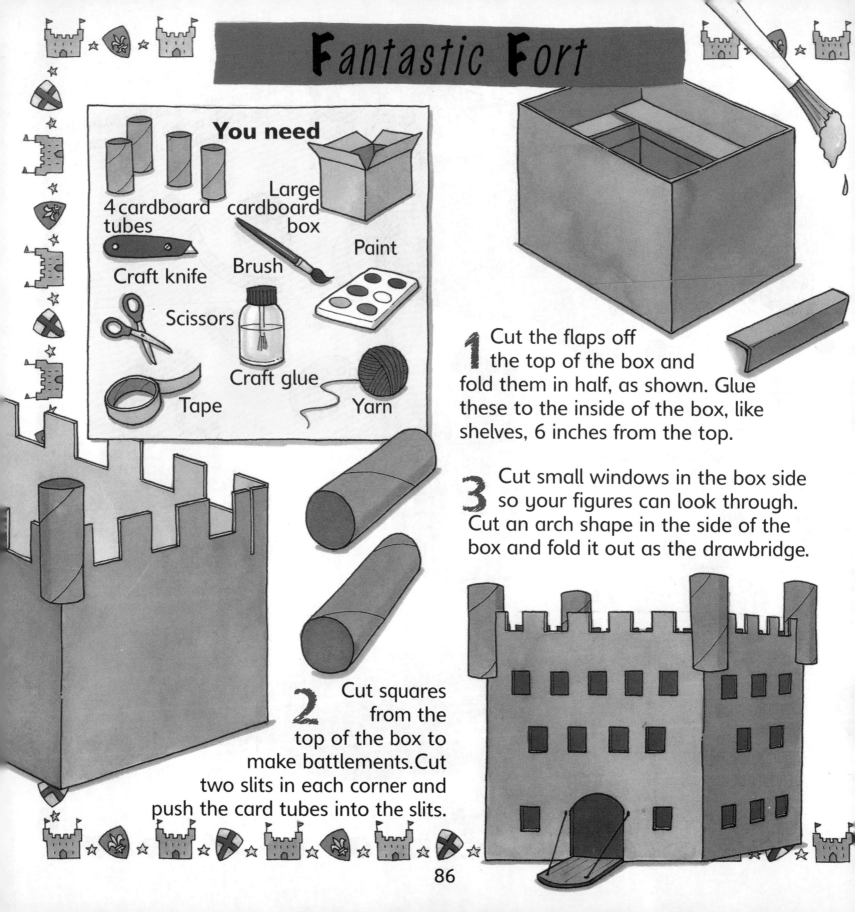

You need

4 cardboard tubes

Large cardboard box

Craft knife

Brush

Paint

Scissors

Craft glue

Tape

Yarn

1 Cut the flaps off the top of the box and fold them in half, as shown. Glue these to the inside of the box, like shelves, 6 inches from the top.

3 Cut small windows in the box side so your figures can look through. Cut an arch shape in the side of the box and fold it out as the drawbridge.

2 Cut squares from the top of the box to make battlements. Cut two slits in each corner and push the card tubes into the slits.

4 Paint your fort and leave it to dry. Then draw on extra windows and stones or bricks with black paint or a felt-tip pen.

Top tip
Make sure you ask an adult to help you cut the holes in the box as the cardboard may be very thick.

Make flags with colored paper and toothpicks.

Use yarn to make chains for the drawbridge.

Terrific Train

You need

Small boxes

Colored paper

Glue

Scissors

Pencil

Card

Small yogurt container

Ruler

2 Glue the two boxes together as shown. Cover the yogurt container with a strip of paper. Snip the paper and fold it over. Glue a circle on top.

1 Glue two empty boxes closed and cover each with colored paper, just like wrapping a present.

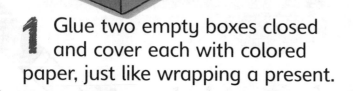

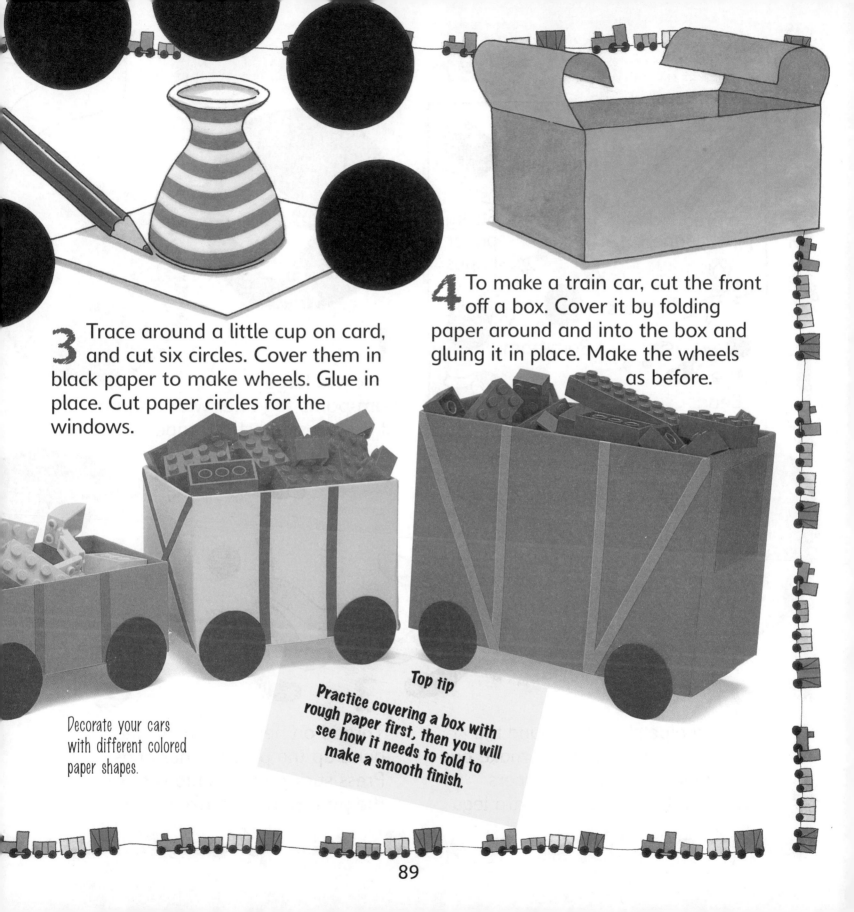

3 Trace around a little cup on card, and cut six circles. Cover them in black paper to make wheels. Glue in place. Cut paper circles for the windows.

4 To make a train car, cut the front off a box. Cover it by folding paper around and into the box and gluing it in place. Make the wheels as before.

Decorate your cars with different colored paper shapes.

Top tip

Practice covering a box with rough paper first, then you will see how it needs to fold to make a smooth finish.

Creepy Critters

You need

Colored pipe cleaners

Thin elastic

Sticky paper shapes

Scissors

Pom-poms

Beads

Double-sided tape

1 Stick two large pom-poms together with a square of double-sided sticky tape.

2 Twist a pipe cleaner around the middle of a pom-pom to make two legs. Twist more pipe cleaners through the first to add extra legs

3 Thread on beads for eyes and bend up the pipe cleaner ends. Press sticky paper shapes onto the pom-pom to make a face.

Top tip
If your creepy critter is really heavy or has a long body, hang it from two pieces of elastic, attached at either end.

4 Now tie thin elastic around the body of your creepy critter and it's ready to hang up.

Use a pipe cleaner to make antennae.

Create your own mini monsters and scare your friends!

Add beads to make feet or just bend the pipe cleaners into shape.

Native Homes

You need

- Cardboard
- 6 large wooden skewers
- Dinner plate
- Craft glue
- Saucer
- Fabric
- Scissors
- Green paper
- Pencil
- Small rubber bands
- Felt-tip pens

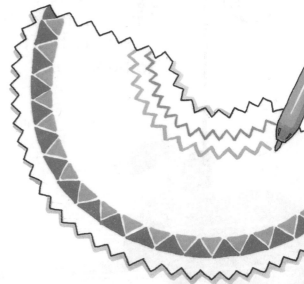

1 Cover the cardboard with green paper. Place the saucer on the board and mark six evenly spaced dots around it with the pencil.

2 Push the pointed ends of the skewers on the dots and into the cardboard. Pull the tops together and wrap a rubber band around.

3 Draw around a dinner plate on the fabric and cut out a semi-circle. Decorate the edges with bright-colored felt-tip pens.

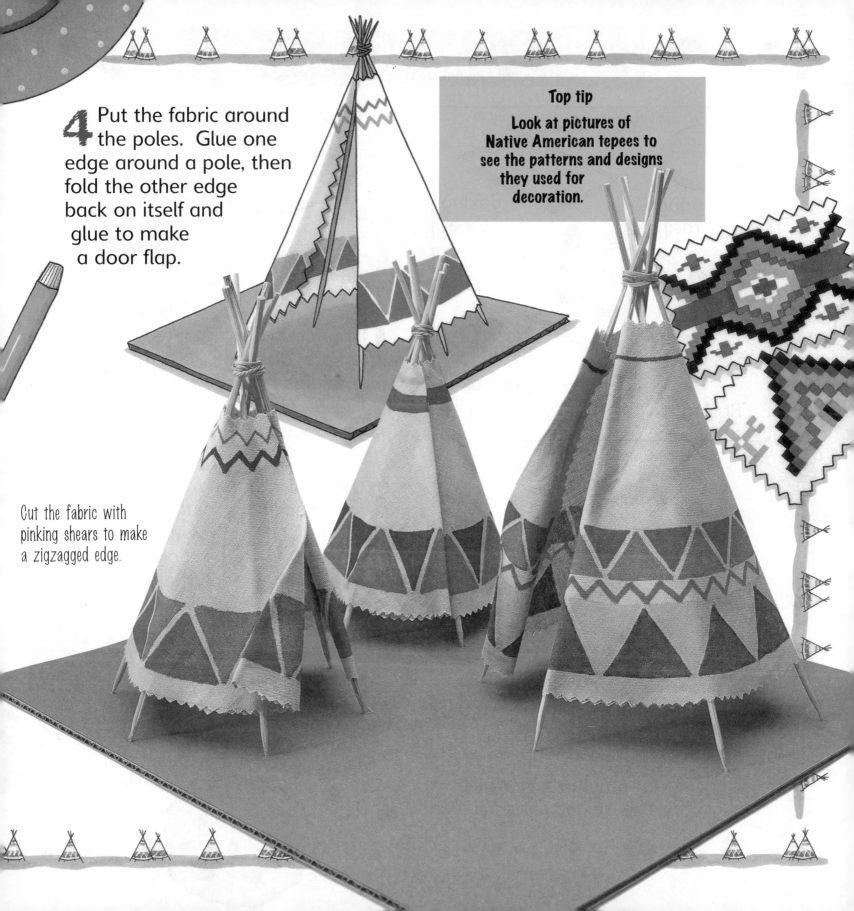

4 Put the fabric around the poles. Glue one edge around a pole, then fold the other edge back on itself and glue to make a door flap.

Top tip

Look at pictures of Native American tepees to see the patterns and designs they used for decoration.

Cut the fabric with pinking shears to make a zigzagged edge.

You need

Salt dough
(see recipe)

Baking sheet

Food coloring

Cookie cutters

Paintbrush

Rolling pin

Blunt knife

Keep the different colored dough in separate containers.

1 Drip food coloring onto a small lump of dough. Roll the dough in your fingers until the color is mixed in. Wash your hands and color some more dough in the same way.

2 To make a bun, roll some dough into a ball, squash it, and cut it in half. Press small pieces of colored dough into the shape of lettuce and cheese and place in a bun.

3 Roll out a small amount of dough and cut circles using cookie cutters. Press tiny balls of brown dough on to make chocolate chip cookies. Cut red heart shapes to decorate the cookies.

Don't roll the dough too thin.

4 For cup cakes, shape the dough first, then add thin pieces of dough as the icing.

Try painting on extra food coloring once you have formed the dough.

5 Place all your dough models on a baking sheet. Ask an adult to help you put this in the oven. Bake for at least two hours at 170°F.

Remember!
Let your models cool before you play with them.

Recipe

2 cups of flour, 1 cup of salt, 1 cup of water, 1 tablespoon of oil

Mix the flour and salt together and add the water and oil. Mix together and knead with your hands, until smooth. Store this in an airtight container in the refrigerator.

More Ideas

1 Draw a face on the bowl of a wooden spoon with a felt-tip pen. Choose another color to draw on the hair.

2 Cut two strips of card and glue them together on either side of the spoon handle. Trim the ends into hand shapes.

Make a shirt in your favorite team's colors!

3 Cut two T-shirt shapes from fabric or paper. Place these on either side of the spoon handle and glue them together at the edges.

Concept: Tony Potter
Photography: Zul Mukhida
Design: Roger O'Hara, Nicky Chapman, Chris Dymond, Kate Buxton, Teresa Foster.
Illustrations: Chris Dymond, Clare Beaton, Kim Woolley.

This edition produced in 1998 by Zigzag Publishing, an imprint of Quadrillion Publishing Ltd., Godalming Business Centre, Godalming, Surrey GU7 1XW, England.

Ref. no. 8512

ISBN 0-7651-0705-8

Printed in France